D1433429

The CHILD'S CHRISTMAS

*To Bruno Bettelheim
for caring and knowing so much about children
and the importance of Santa Claus*

The CHILD'S CHRISTMAS

Edited and introduced by
ANNE WOOD

Blackie

ACKNOWLEDGEMENTS

The Publishers would like to thank the following copyright holders for their permission to reproduce the copyright material in this book:

David Higham Associates for 'For Them', 'Welcome to the New Year', 'Wake Up!', 'Up the Hill, Down the Hill' and the extract from *The Glass Peacock* by Eleanor Farjeon and for the extract from *Christmas with the Savages* by Mary Clive; Stanley Cook for 'Christmas Trees'; Macmillan Publishers for the extract from *The Christmas Book* by Enid Blyton; Friendly Press for the extract from *A Ridiculous Idea* by Elizabeth M. Wilton; *The Father Christmas Letter* by J. R. R. Tolkein Reprinted by permission of George Allen & Unwin (Publishers) Ltd © 1976 and Houghton Mifflin Co.; Faber & Faber Ltd for the extract from *The Country Child* by Alison Uttley; A. P. Watt Publishers Inc. on behalf of Miss D. E. Collins for 'How Far is it to Bethlehem?' by Frances Chesterton; Lutterworth Press and Harper & Row for the extract from *Farmer Boy* by Laura Ingalls Wilder; 'The Christmas Wish' from *The Little Christmas Book* by Rose Fyleman © 1927 by George H. Doran, reprinted by permission of The Society of Authors Ltd and Doubleday, a division of Bantam, Doubleday, Dell Publishing Group Inc.; Chappell Music for ' "I," said the Donkey' Traditional/adapted by Christopher Rowe.

Every attempt has been made to trace the copyright holders of the poems in this book. The Publishers apologize if any inadvertent omissions have been made.

The Editor would like to thank Sara Conkey and Carole Thomson, friends and co-workers on this book.

The publishers and editor would like to thank
Fine Art Developments PLC for making available their resources
of Victorian Christmas cards which form the
colour plates in this book.

Copyright © in this collection Anne Wood 1988
Cover illustrations by kind permission of Fine Art Developments PLC
First published 1988 by Blackie and Son Ltd

British Library Cataloguing in Publication Data available

Blackie and Son Ltd
7 Leicester Place
London WC2H 7BP

Printed in Great Britain by Thomson Litho
Designed by Karen Stafford

Contents

Introduction

When I was invited to submit a substitute text for Charles Robinson's book, first published in 1906, I was immediately won over by the sumptuous look and feel of Charles Robinson's original illustrations and book design.

I soon discovered that Charles Robinson's belief in Christmas and Santa Claus as a symbol of all good things was as complete as his children's. The father of six, four girls and two boys, he enjoyed the lavish family parties, the visits to the pantomime and other child-centred Christmas rituals as much as they did. There could have been no exclusive atmosphere in the Robinson household. Charles frequently had children playing or drawing at his feet as he worked and *The Child's Christmas* reflected life in his own home.

The original text was by Evelyn Sharp, leading suffragette, sister of Cecil Sharp, the folklorist, and a guest at the Robinson's wedding who would have observed the Robinson children at first-hand from their earliest years. We have kept enough of her text to give a flavour of what life might have been like for those lucky children in a secure Edwardian family. But times have changed and so we also sought thoughts on Christmas by today's children in their own words. A competition organized by the Books for Children club gave us 'Dog in a Box' from Andrew Jackson aged five, 'Where *do* you put the Christmas Tree?' from Karen Cameron aged eight, and 'Santa's New Sleigh' from Jonathan Hill aged eleven.

As for the rest there are very familiar stories and rhymes by Hans Andersen and Eleanor Farjeon, some less familiar like J. R. R. Tolkien's letters from Santa Claus and an episode from that foremost of all Christmas books *Christmas With The Savages* by Mary Clive. There are also stories and rhymes that would have delighted children even before the little Robinsons were a gleam in their father's eye. For 'so hallowed and so gracious is the time' of Christmas that it has always belonged to children. A special holiday, celebrating the birth of a baby makes them feel welcome and wanted. As for the conspiracy that is Santa Claus, it is an invitation to adults, too, to indulge in wishes even though we know they can't always come true.

Something of all this we have tried to capture in this book which should be brought out every year and dipped into for reading aloud, a sliver at a time, as the season approaches.

HAPPY CHRISTMAS.

ANNE WOOD

Buying Presents

Evelyn Sharp

There was a clatter on the nursery floor, and three empty money-boxes stood beside three heaps of pennies. Nancy's was the biggest heap, and Elfie's was the second biggest, and Pat's was the smallest.

'I do wish I had not spent so much money on toffee, last week' sighed Pat.

'That comes of being greedy,' said Nurse, who never lost an opportunity of this sort. 'Now, make haste and get ready, or we shall not finish our shopping before dinner-time.'

Then Baby, who had no money-box, was given a penny to hold, and the whole family set out for the town to buy presents. Father and Mother came too, so when they were all inside the first shop there was scarcely room to move. But the shopman did not seem to mind.

'The more the merrier,' he said; and Elfie wondered why people always said that, when there was such a crowd that she could not see anything but legs and elbows. Then the shopman lifted her on to a chair, and they all began to choose Christmas cards. It was very exciting, because, of course, nobody wanted anybody else to see what cards were being bought, and it was not easy in such a small shop to buy them in private. Still, the shopman was very obliging, and that was a great help.

Then they all came out of that shop and went on to the most important shop in the town, which, of course, was a toy-shop. It was covered all over with toys; they hung from the roof and they lay about the floor; it was quite difficult to walk without stepping on them.

'Which toy do you like best, Baby?' asked Mother.

'I like them all best,' said Baby. But when Nurse explained that at Christmas time people bought toys for other people, he held out a hot penny and said: 'A present for Nancy, please.'

The Glass Peacock

ELEANOR FARJEON

Christmas drew near, and the little shops in Mellin's Court began to look happy. The sweetstuff shop had a Fairy Doll in white muslin and tinsel in the middle of the window, and some paper festoons and cheap toys appeared among the glass bottles. At the greengrocer's, a sort of glorified open stall which overflowed into the courtyard, evergreens and pineapples appeared, and on one magic morning Christmas trees. The grocery window at the corner had already blossomed into dates and figs and candied fruits, and blue-and-white jars of ginger; and the big confectioner's in the High Street had in the window, as well as puddings in basins, a Christmas Cake a yard square – a great flat frosted 'set piece', covered with robins, windmills, snow babies, and a scarlet Santa Claus with a sled full of tiny toys. This cake would presently be cut up and sold by the pound, and you got the attractions on top 'as you came' – oh lucky, lucky buyer-to-be of the Santa Claus sled! The children of Mellin's Court were already choosing their favourite toys and cakes and fruits from the rich windows, and Annar-Mariar and Willyum chose like all the rest. Of course, they never *thought* they could have the Fairy Queen, the Christmas tree, the big box of sugary fruits, or the marvellous cake – but how they *dreamed* they could! As Christmas drew nearer, smaller hopes of what it would actually bring began to take shape in the different homes. Bobby's mother had *told* him he'd better hang his stocking up on Christmas Eve 'and see'. That meant something. And the Goodenoughs were going to be sent a hamper. And Mabel Baker was going to be taken to the Pantomime! And the Jacksons were all going to their Granny's in Lambeth for a party. And this child and that had so much, or so little, in the Sweet Club.

And as Christmas drew nearer, it became plainer and plainer to Annar-Mariar that this year, for one reason or another, Christmas wasn't going to bring her and Willyum anything. And it didn't. Up to the last they got *their* treat from the shop-windows, and did all their shopping there. Annar-Mariar never stinted her Christmas Window-shopping.

'What'll *you* 'ave, Willyum? I'll 'ave the Fairy Queen, I think. Would you like them trains?'

'Ss!' said Willyum. 'And I'd like the Fairy Queen.'

'Orl right. You 'ave her. I'll 'ave that music box.'

At the confectioner's: 'Shall we 'ave a big puddin' for us both, or a little puddin' each, Willyum?'

'A big puddin' each,' said Willyum.

'Orl right. And them red crackers with the gold bells on, and I'll tell 'em to send the big cake round too, shall I?'

'Ss!' said Willyum, 'and I'll 'ave the Farver Crismuss.'

'Orl right, ducks. You can.'

And at the grocer's Willyum had the biggest box of candied fruits, and at the greengrocer's the biggest pineapple. He agreed, however, to a single tree – the biggest between them, and under Annar-Mariar's lavish disregard of money there was plenty of everything for them both, and for anybody who cared to 'drop in' on Christmas Day.

May Christmas be happy

'"Which toy do you like best, Baby?" asked Mother.
"I like them all best," said Baby.'

EVELYN SHARP

'There is a great deal to do on Christmas Eve
in the afternoon. For one thing, there are
all the cards to be addressed . . .'

EVELYN SHARP

Dog in a Box

ALEXANDER JACKSON (AGE 5)

I am a dog in a box
Like a homeless fox
Nobody wants me.
Boys want monster machines,
Girls want dolls,
Babies want nappies.
I am stuck on the shelf
All night and day
Never have anyone to play.
I want to be dusted by an elf
Wrapped up and put on to a sleigh.
I will be opened on Christmas Day
By excited children
Who will want to play
With me
And cuddle me in bed all night
Until it's light.

Maid Bess

A Christmas Ballad

ANNA ROBESON BROWN

One Christmas Eve: (so the List'ner heard),
During the reign of George the Third,
Over the road to Willoughby Hall.
Under the beeches, stiff and tall,
The Squire's coach, and his horses brown,
Bore their master from London Town:
From London Town, where a week before
The coach had stopped at a palace door,
And poor John Peter, in waistcoat fine,
Had sat and gaped at Queen Caroline.

Now, from the Court where people press,
The Squire, his wife, and their daughter Bess,
Weary, perchance, yet merry withal,
Were on their way home to Willoughby Hall.
The Squire was testy, and toss'd about,
Grumbled because his pipe was out.
My Lady's sleep was placid and sound,
And visions came, as the wheels went round
(Visions that stay'd when dreams were gone),
Of a purple silk and a gay sprigged lawn.

Bess, in her mantle of paduasoy,
Hugg'd to her bosom a fine new toy –
A slender whip with a silver head,
To startle her pony, dappled 'Ned'.
Now with each passing white mile-stone
The little maiden had gayer grown,
Till, in spite of the bitter freeze,
She begged 'to sit by the coachman, please!'
So with joy at her novel ride,
Prattled and laughed at John Peter's side.

Sudden, from out the trees near by
Standing dark 'gainst the sunset sky,
Six black figures on horseback sped
Close on the coach. Ere a word was said,
A pistol was cocked, and a voice cried, 'Stop!'
(Poor John Peter was ready to drop,
Cried out 'Mercy!' and made such a fuss
They threatened him with a blunderbuss!)
The Squire, he blustered; the Lady screamed –
Something had happen'd that nobody dreamed:
Nobody thought they should have to fight
Six great robbers that very night,
Even though, just the week before,
Highwaymen halted a coach-and-four!

The Squire was gagged ere his sword was out,
All the packets were tumbled about;
The footman ran without staying to fight;
Poor John Peter was stiff with fright!
The Lady fainted in dire distress.
Nobody thought very much about Bess –
She had not stirred, nor screamed, nor made
Sign to show that she felt afraid;
But safe in her place, she bolder grew,
For the wise little maid saw what to do.

The robbers were careless, sure of success
(Nobody counted on little Bess).
She, who saw while the moments sped
A robber moved from the horse's head,
Seized the whip, pushed the coachman back,
Hit 'Brown Jerry' a sounding thwack!
Up went his nose with a snort of scorn
(This is how it was told next morn),
Flung out his hoof (so the papers said),
Hit a robber and broke his head!
Then was off with the speed of the wind,
Leaving the robbers all behind!
Off like mad o'er the snowy course,
Ere a robber could mount his horse!

How My Lady hugged Bess and sobbed!
How John Peter told who was robbed!
How the Squire, with pride and glee,
Cried, 'She did for 'em, trouncingly!'
How old Janet, the nurse, cried 'Jack!
What a marcy ye all came back!'
How maid Bess, at her father's side,
Carved the pudding at Christmas-tide –
The great big pudding with every plum
Worthy of little Jack Horner's thumb!
How her grandam and cousins five
Pledged her 'the pluckiest girl alive.'
The longest words could not tell it all,
The joy and the laughter: at Willoughby Hall.

Addressing the Cards

EVELYN SHARP

CHARLES ROBINSON

There is a great deal to do on Christmas Eve in the afternoon. For one thing, there are all the cards to be addressed, and this cannot be done without a great deal of patience and a great deal of ink. Baby used up more ink than anybody; though he did not know how to write. But Nancy held his hand and guided it over his Christmas card so that he wrote in big shaky letters – 'To Mother from Baby.' Then he felt very proud of himself, and put his finger in the ink-pot and sucked it to see if the black would come off. It did come off, and the taste was very nasty. 'I don't like writing,' said Baby, as Nurse carried him off to be washed.

Elfie could not write, either; but she knew how to print capital letters, so she printed the words as Nancy spelt them to her. Unfortunately, Nancy forgot to tell her where the words ended, so when the card was addressed it looked like this –

TOMOTHERFROMELFIE

But mothers always understand that kind of writing; so it did not matter.

Pat knew how to write, so he addressed his cards by himself. He shook the whole table when he wrote. He curled one leg tightly round his chair, and with the other he kicked everybody within reach. He wrote with his mouth wide open and his nose very close to the envelope, and a good deal of ink went on his face by mistake. He would not let Nancy help him because he knew how to write, and when he had finished, this is what he had written –

to mother. wishing her a merry Christmass.

'I am glad we do not have cards to address every day,' said Nancy, when she at last had a moment's peace in which to address her own.

'It is quite easy when you know how,' said Pat in a superior tone.

Christmas Trees

STANLEY COOK

The Christmas trees in the forest
Stand in a long row,
Spreading their branches like arms
To catch the falling snow.

Their branches point at the moon
And the stars in the sky
And reach to catch the clouds
That go floating by.

When they come indoors
They gather in their arms
Christmas presents and tinsel
And hold bright lights and stars.

The Christmas Tree

Enid Blyton

'Mother, who thought of the first Christmas tree? It's such a good idea.'

'It is, isn't it,' said Mother, cutting some coloured string into small pieces, so that she might tie small presents on the tree. 'Well, I don't exactly know who thought of the first Christmas tree, as *we* know it – but there is rather a nice old story about it.'

'Tell us, please!' said Ann, who loved a story of any kind.

'Well,' said Mother, 'one stormy Christmas Eve, long long ago, a forester and his family were sitting together round a big fire. Outside, the wind blew, and the snow made the forest white.

Suddenly there came a knock at the door. The family looked up, startled. "Who can be in the forest at this time of the night?" said the forester, in surprise, and got up to open the door.

Outside stood a little child, shivering with cold, tired and hungry. The forester picked him up in amazement, and brought him into the warm room.

"See," he said, "it is a little child. Who can he be?"

"He must remain here for the night," said his wife, feeling the child's ice-cold hands. "We will give him hot milk to drink, and a bed to sleep in."

"He can have my bed," said Hans, the forester's son. "I can sleep on the floor tonight. Let us put the child into my warm bed."

So the hungry, cold child was fed and warmed, and put into Hans' bed for the night. Then the family went to sleep, Hans on the floor beside the fire.

In the morning the forester awoke, and heard an astonishing sound. It seemed to him as if a whole choir of voices was singing. He awoke his wife, and she too heard the sweet singing.

"It is like the singing of angels," whispered the forester. Then they looked at the child they had sheltered for the night, and saw that his face was dazzling bright. He was the Christ-Child Himself!

In awe and wonder the forester and his family watched the Holy Child. He went to a fir-tree, and broke off a branch. He planted the branch firmly in the ground.

"See," he said, "you were kind to me, and you gave me the gifts of warmth and food and shelter. Now here is my gift to you – a tree that at Christmas time shall bear its fruit, so that you may always have abundance."

And so, at Christmas time, the Christmas tree shines out in beauty, and bears gifts of many kinds.'

Where Do You Put the Christmas Tree?

Karen Cameron (aged 8)

In our house we never agree
On where to put the Christmas tree.
Every year it is the same
We cannot put it there again!
In the corner beside the wall
What about out in the hall?
Next to the piano or kitchen door
Somewhere in the middle of the floor?
Oh how great it would be
To know where to put the Christmas tree.

A Christmas Tree

CHARLES DICKENS

The tree was planted in the middle of a great round table, and towered high above their heads. It was brilliantly lighted by a multitude of little tapers; and everywhere sparkled and glittered with bright objects. There were rosy-cheeked dolls, hiding behind the green leaves; and there were real watches (with movable hands, at least, and an endless capacity of being wound up) dangling from innumerable twigs; there were French-polished tables, chairs, bedsteads, wardrobes, eight-day clocks, and various other articles of domestic furniture (wonderfully made, in tin, at Wolverhampton), perched among the boughs, as if in preparation for some fairy housekeeping; there were jolly, broad-faced little men, much more agreeable in appearance than many real men – and no wonder, for their heads took off and showed them to be full of sugar-plums; there were fiddles and drums; there were tambourines, books, work-boxes, paint-boxes; there were trinkets for the elder girls far brighter than any grown-up gold and jewels; there were baskets and pincushions in all devices; there were guns, swords and banners; there were witches standing in enchanted rings of pasteboard to tell fortunes; there were tee-totums, humming-tops, needle-cases, pen-wipers, smelling bottles, conversation-cards, bouquet-holders; real fruit, made artificially dazzling with gold leaf; imitation apples, pears and walnuts crammed with surprises; in short, as a pretty child, before me, delightedly whispered to another pretty child, her bosom friend, 'There was everything and more.'

COME·BRING·WITH·A·NOISE·MY·MERRY·MERRY·BOYS·THE·CHRISTMAS·LOG·TO·THE·FIRING·

ALL·CHRISTMAS·JOYS·BE·THINE·

'And the first tree in the greenwood
It was the holly.'

SANS DAY CAROL

'Silent Night, Holy Night
All is calm, all is bright.'

A Story Told on Christmas Eve

Elizabeth M. Wilton

'Long, long and very long ago,' Tom began, 'there lived a bad tempered old woman named Eila. Her face was all criss-crossed with lines, she had forgotten how to smile, and all the people of the village were afraid of her. They called her a witch. No one would ever go near her cottage in case she put a spell on them.

'Now one year, there came a very hard winter. For days and days it snowed until the people could not even get outside to find wood for their fires. On Christmas night there was smoke from only one chimney in the village – Eila's. A blizzard was raging outside; an icy wind howled around the cottages, shaking the casements and finding its way in through every little chink. The villagers went shivering to bed, and prayed for the winter to end. When they saw the smoke from Eila's chimney they were afraid – and whispered that she must have called the powers of darkness to her aid; for how could anyone get wood in such a storm?

'Meanwhile, Eila sat cosily before her fire, listening to the wind shrieking outside. Suddenly she thought she heard another sound. Impatiently she shook her head, thinking she must be mistaken. Who would knock at old Eila's door? Who indeed? It must be the wind, she thought.

'But the sound came again. Eila shook her head, but she got stiffly to her feet, and cautiously unbolted the door. The wind tore it from her grasp, flinging it wide. A child stood there on the threshold. He was barefooted in all the snow, his face was pinched and white with cold.

'"My fire has gone out," he said, "let me take a stick from yours."

'Eila was so astonished that for a moment she said nothing. "Have you forgotten who I am?" she asked at last. "I'm Eila. Eila the witch. Get you hence, child; Eila gives nothing to anyone." She slammed the door shut, and returned grumbling to her fire.

'But that night Eila could not sleep. She kept remembering the child, and his pinched white face.

'"He was barefooted, too," she cried aloud, "and in all that snow! I must find him, and give him my fire."

'At once she got up and dressed. Taking a burning stick from the fire and a bundle of faggots to replenish it, she went out into the storm, down the road to the village. She knocked on the door of every house. The villagers were amazed when they saw her, but to her question they all shook their heads.

'"No, we have not seen the child. He does not belong here."

'At each house she kindled a faggot from her burning stick, and gave it to the villager.

'"Light your fire," she said, "in case he comes here."

'And always, though she gave away so many, the bundle of faggots seemed to stay as large as before.

'All over the country Eila wandered, in search of the child, giving her fire wherever the coals in some cottage were dead. And strangely, with every faggot she gave away, one of the lines in her face went too, until it was as smooth and beautiful as a young girl's.

'At last, after many years of searching, she returned to her own village. That Christmas was another as bitter as the one when the child knocked at her door. But this time there was no fire on Eila's hearth, for in spite of her youthful face, she was too old to go and gather sticks for herself. As she sat there, shivering and listening to the wind, there came a knock, just as before. She opened the door. There stood the child.

'"Alack, little one," she cried, "why have you come to me now, when I have no fire to give you?"

'The child smiled and drawing Eila out into the road, pointed to the village. In every house was the warm glow of fire.

'"When you have none to give me?" said the child. "Why, Eila, every fire you have kindled has been for me."

'Then Eila looked at him again. He was barefooted in the snow, but he was not pinched and cold. He was as warm as if he were in a firelit room.

'"Why," she gasped, "Thou art the Christ Child."

'So,' said Tom, finishing the story, 'from that day to this, every villager at home puts a candle in his window on Christmas night, in case the Christ Child should come, as he did to Eila so long ago.'

The Great Secret

EVELYN SHARP

'Pat,' said Nancy in a loud whisper, 'go and see if all is safe.'

Pat crept on tiptoe to the top of the stairs and came back to say that no one was in sight. Nancy went to the night nursery cupboard and brought out a brown paper parcel, and they all stood round in their night-gowns. Then the paper was taken off, and they had a last look at the present they had bought for Father and Mother. It was a picture of the children, Baby and all, framed in red leather; and it was a tremendous surprise, for no one but Nurse even knew that it had been taken.

'I hope Mother won't notice that Baby screwed up his mouth,' said Pat.

'I hope Father will see how well Sophia has come out,' said Nancy.

'Doesn't my new frock look pretty?' said Elfie.

Then the picture was put back again into the brown paper, and not a moment too soon; for just then, there came a step on the landing, and Mother came right into the room. However, she did not seem to notice anything unusual, though Pat rushed to the cupboard in a great hurry, and the two girls looked very red in the face.

'You did not hear anything funny, did you, Mother?' enquired Elfie.

'I can hear Baby splashing in his bath,' said Mother; and this was a great relief to everyone. Baby, in his bath, made far more noise than any brown paper parcel.

Hanging up the Stockings

EVELYN SHARP

Going to bed becomes a pleasure on Christmas Eve, because, as everybody knows, bed makes the next day come quicker. Besides, there are the stockings to hang up.

'I wonder if the biggest stockings get the most presents,' said Pat.

'I hope not,' said Elfie, looking at her own, which were the shortest.

'The best children get the most presents,' said Nurse.

'Are we best children?' wondered Pat, anxiously.

'That depends on whether we are written in Santa Claus's Book of Good Children,' said Nancy.

'Oh dear,' sighed Pat. 'I hit Baby on the head for bursting my new airball, yesterday.'

Elfie ran to the chimney and called up it as loudly as she could: 'Please, Santa Claus, leave your Book of Bad Children at home, and don't forget my dolly with the blue eyes.'

Cousin Bob, who was big enough to do his own hair and compound long divisions, burst out laughing. 'You funny children!' he cried. 'Do you mean to say that you believe in Santa Claus?'

There was complete silence in the night nursery when Cousin Bob said this. The children were too surprised to speak at first. Then Elfie looked over her shoulder, and said in a shocked tone: 'Oh, hush, Bob! Something dreadful will happen to you if you talk like that.'

'I don't care,' said Bob. But he felt a little uneasy, all the same.

How the Cat kept Christmas

(FROM THE NEW YEAR'S BARGAIN BY SUSAN COOLIDGE)

Off they went, the magic stillness of the night broken only by the tinkling bells. First one chimney, then another; bag after bag full of toys and sweets; here a doll, there a diamond ring, here only a pair of warm stockings. Everybody had something, except in a few houses over whose roofs St Nicholas paused a moment with a look half sad, half angry, and left nothing. People lived there who knew him little, and loved him less.

Through the air – more towns – more villages. Now the sea was below them, the cold, moon-lit sea. Then again land came in sight – towers and steeples, halls and hamlets; and the work began again. A wild longing seized the Cat. She begged the Saint to take her down one specially wide chimney on his shoulder. He did so. The nursery within looked strange and foreign; but the little sleeping face in bed was like Gretchen's and pussy felt at home. A whole bag full of presents was left here . . .

And then, hey! presto! they were off again to countless homes, to roofs so poor and low that only a Saint would have thought of visiting them, to

stately palaces, to cellars and toll-gates and lonely attics; at last to a church, dim, and fragrant with ivy-leaves and twisted evergreen, where their errand was to feed a robin who had found shelter, and was sleeping on the topmost bough. How his beads of eyes sparkled as the Saint awoke him! and how eagerly he pecked the store of good red berries which were *his* Christmas present, though he had hung up no stocking and evidently expected nothing.

What Willie Wants

ANON

Dear Santa Claus
You brought a sled
To me a year ago
And when you come again I hope
You'll bring along some snow

Santa Claus and the Mouse

EMILIE POULSSON

One Christmas eve, when Santa Claus
    Came to a certain house,
To fill the children's stockings there,
    He found a little mouse.

'A merry Christmas, little friend,'
    Said Santa, good and kind
'The same to you, sir,' said the mouse;
    'I thought you wouldn't mind

'If I should stay awake tonight
    And watch you for a while.'
'You're very welcome, little mouse,'
    Said Santa, with a smile.

'Blow your fingers, stamp your toes
Don't let Jack Frost nip your nose
Up the hill and down again
Lots of fun for little men.'

'Away in a manger,
No crib for a bed.'

And then he filled the stockings up
    Before the mouse could wink –
From toe to top, from top to toe,
    There wasn't left a chink.

'Now, they won't hold another thing,'
    Said Santa Claus, with pride.
A twinkle came in mouse's eyes,
    But humbly he replied:

'It's not polite to contradict –
    Your pardon I implore –
But in the fullest stocking there
    I could put one thing more.'

'Oh, ho!' laughed Santa, 'silly mouse!
    Don't I know how to pack?
By filling stockings all these years.
    I should have learned the knack.'

And then he took the stocking
    From where it hung so high,
And said: 'Now put in one thing more;
    I give you leave to try.'

The mousie chuckled to himself,
    And then he softly stole
Right to the stocking's crowded toe
    And gnawed a little hole!

'Now if you please, good Santa Claus.
    I've put in one thing more;
For you will own that little hole
    Was not in there before.'

How Santa Claus did laugh and laugh!
    And then he gravely spoke:
'Well! you shall have a Christmas cheese
    For that nice little joke.'

The 1925 Father Christmas Letter

J. R. R. TOLKEIN

I am dreadfully busy this year – it makes my hand more shaky than ever when I think of it – and not very rich. In fact, awful things have been happening, and some of the presents have got spoilt and I haven't got the North Polar Bear to help me and I have had to move house just before Christmas, so you can imagine what a state everything is in, and you will see why I have a new address. It all happened like this: one very windy day last November my hood blew off and went and stuck on the top of the North Pole. I told him not to, but the North Polar Bear climbed up to the thin top to get it down – and he did. The pole broke in the middle and fell on the roof of my house, and the North Polar Bear fell through the hole it made into the dining room with my hood over his nose, and all the snow fell off the roof into the house and melted and put out all the fires and ran down into the cellars where I was collecting this year's presents, and the North Polar Bear's leg got broken. He is well again now, but I was so cross with him that he says he won't try to help me again. I expect his temper is hurt, and will be mended by next Christmas. I send you a picture of the accident, and of my new house on the cliffs above the North Pole (with beautiful cellars in the cliffs). If John can't read my old shaky writing (1925 years old) he must get his father to. When is Michael going to learn to read, and write his own letters to me? Lots of love to you both and Christopher, whose name is rather like mine.

Santa's New Sleigh

JONATHAN HILL (AGE 11)

It was the 23rd of December. At the North Pole Santa and his dwarfs were preparing for the next day. The dwarfs had been making and buying toys and they were now almost finished. It was time to prepare the sleigh. Noggin, the head dwarf, ran up to Santa.

'The sleigh's collapsed!' he wailed. 'It's full of woodworm. We can't use it.'

Santa leapt up. 'What!' he cried. 'What do you mean?'

He ran out to the stables. The reindeer were nosing around at a pile of painted wood that looked as though a hefty elephant had sat on it. The dwarfs were just standing there unhappily.

'This is awful,' moaned Santa. 'Where can we get another one? There are no spares. Can't we cut down our trees and make one?'

'But they've got a very rare willow disease.'

'What! They're oaks!'

'It's very rare.'

Santa sat down. 'Let's see. We can't use the old sleigh. We can't make another. Got it!' He leapt up. 'Here, Noggin, how about that firm you got the toy robots from? They must have some sort of power-sleighs.'

'Good idea!' said Noggin. A dwarf ran off to the phone. Within two minutes he was back.

'They say, yes, they've got this sort of flying jet sleigh. It's got bells and everything,' he said.

'Fantastic!' said Santa. 'Now we have to wait.' They all went indoors to the huge workshop. Noggin waited outside. A few minutes later he ran back in again.

'It's here! It's here!' he shouted. Everyone ran out.

They saw a large metal thing on runners. It had jets at the back, headlights and indicators. A dwarf patted it and it shook violently.

'I-I'm not going i-in that!' stammered Santa.

'Nonsense!' said Noggin. 'You'll love it. Come on, boys, pack 'er up.'

Next afternoon Santa sat nervously in the sleigh. It looked very complicated. As the dwarfs loaded the last of the presents, he tried a few of the controls. The heater came on.

'OK,' called Noggin. 'Ready, you can go now.'

Santa gulped. He turned the key, accelerated and was off in a wave of glitter and noise. The sleigh circled the warehouse twice, then rushed off as Santa recovered his breath.

He reached England in minutes. He managed to quieten the sleigh, so he could land. After years of practice it was possible for him to do a house in ten seconds. One time he left the motor running and only just managed to catch hold of the flying sleigh.

Then he went on to all the other countries.

As he came back to the North Pole, the engine spluttered and coughed. The sleigh dipped, then careered round the warehouse, through the terrified dwarfs and into a deep snowdrift. As the dwarfs dug him out, Santa said,

'You know, there's a lot to be said for progress, but I think I like the old methods best.

A Letter from Santa Claus

(FROM CHRISTMAS POEMS AND STORIES FOR VERY LITTLE ONES, 1890)

My dear Carl,

I love you so much that I must write you a few words, though I really hardly have time. My reindeer team are pawing with their little hoofs, and the wind is so high that I'm afraid half my toys will be blown away; and then what will the children say?

I filled the stockings that were hung up in Boston first, and then I came very fast overland, filling all the stockings as I came along. After San Francisco was well supplied, I had to cross the Pacific Ocean, to get to you in Honolulu. I had been riding in a sleigh; but now I harnessed my reindeer to a little boat, and they swam over here very fast. When we were nearly here, we passed a big steamer, and I went close to it to see who was there. I found one gentleman who was thinking of his little boys and loving them very much and longing to get home to them. I saw, peeping out of his coat pocket, two little cannon; and just then I heard him say, 'I wonder if I shall get home to Ernest and Carl and Kenneth and Baby on Christmas day!' I was just about to shout out, 'Oh, I know your boys, and I'll tell them you are coming!' when my reindeer began to swim very fast indeed, and, before I knew it, I was out of sight of the steamer. When your papa comes, ask him if he saw a funny little man sailing away very fast.

Goodbye, dear.

Your loving friend

Santa Claus

The Country Child

ALISON UTTLEY

Outside under the stars she could see the group of men and women with lanterns throwing beams across the paths and on to the stable door. One man stood apart beating time, another played a fiddle, and another had a flute. The rest sang in four parts the Christmas hymns, 'While Shepherds Watched', 'Come All Ye Faithful', and 'Hark, the Herald angels Sing'.

There was the star. Susan could see it twinkling and bright in the dark boughs with their white frosted layers, and there was the stable. She watched the faces lit up by the lanterns, top-coats pulled up to their necks. The music of the violin came thin and squeaky, like a singing icicle, blue and cold, but magic, and the flute was warm like the voices.

They stopped and waited a moment. Tom's deep voice came from the darkness. They trooped, chattering and puffing out their cheeks, and clapping their arms round their bodies to the front door. They were going in the parlour for elderberry wine and their collection money. A bright light flickered across the snow as the door was flung wide open. Then a bang and Susan went back to bed.

A Christmas Visitor

ANON

He comes in the night! he comes in the night!
    He softly, silently comes;
While the little brown heads on the pillows so white
    Are dreaming of bugles and drums.

He cuts through the snow like a ship through the foam,
    While the white flakes around him whirl;
Who tells him I know not, but he findeth the home
    Of each good little boy and girl.

His sleigh it is long, and deep, and wide;
    It will carry a host of things,
While dozens of drums hang over the side,
    With the sticks sticking under the strings.

And yet not the sound of a drum is heard,
    Not a bugle blast is blown,
As he mounts to the chimney-top like a bird,
    And drops to the hearth like a stone.

The little red stockings he silently fills,
    Till the stockings will hold no more;
The bright little sleds for the great snow hills
    Are quickly set down on the floor.

Then Santa Claus mounts to the roof like a bird,
    And glides to his seat in the sleigh;
Not the sound of a bugle or drum is heard
    As he noiselessly gallops away.

He rides to the East, and he rides to the West,
    Of his goodies he touches not one;
He eateth the crumbs of the Christmas feast
    When the dear little folks are done.

Old Santa Claus doeth all that he can;
    This beautiful mission is his;
Then, children, be good to the little old man
    When you find who the little man is.

How Far is it to Bethlehem?

FRANCES CHESTERTON

How far is it to Bethlehem?
Not very far.
Shall we find the stable room lit by a star?
Can we see the little child, is he within?
If we lift the wooden latch, may we go in?

May we stroke the creatures there,
Ox, ass or sheep?
May we peep like them and see Jesus asleep?
If we touch his tiny hand, will he awake?
Will he know we've come so far just for his sake.

Great kings have precious gifts, and we have naught.
Little smiles and little tears are all we brought.
For all weary children Mary must weep,
Here on his bed of straw, sleep, children, sleep.

'How far is it to Bethlehem?'
FRANCES CHESTERTON

' "I," said the donkey, all shaggy and brown.'

Traditional

'I,' said the Donkey

TRADITIONAL/ADAPTED BY CHRISTOPHER ROWE

'I,' said to the donkey, all shaggy and brown,
'Carried his mother all into the town,
Carried her uphill, carried her down.
I,' said the donkey, all shaggy and brown.

'I,' said the cow, with spots of red,
'Gave him hay for to rest his head,
Gave a manger for his bed.
I,' said the cow, with spots of red.

'I,' said the sheep, with twisted horn,
'Gave my wool for to keep him warm,
Gave my coat on Christmas morn.
I,' said the sheep with twisted horn.

'I,' said the dove from the rafters high,
'Cooed him to sleep with a lullaby,
Cooed him to sleep my mate and I.
I,' said the dove from the rafters high.

If Christ Were Born in Burnley

A. F. BAYLY

If Christ were born in Burnley
    This Christmas night,
    This Christmas night;
I know not if the moors would shine
    With heav'nly light,
    With heav'nly light.
But this I know,
My heart would glow
And all its inner radiance show,
If Christ were born in Burnley.

If Christ were born in Burnley
    This Christmas-tide,
    This Christmas-tide;
I know not if with treasures rare
    The wise would ride,
    The wise would ride.
But I would bring
My offering,
To kneel and worship hastening;
If Christ were born in Burnley.

If Christ were born in Burnley
　　This Christmas day,
　　This Christmas day;
I know not if the busy throng
　　Would bid Him stay,
　　Would bid Him stay.
But He might rest,
My heart's own guest,
Of praise and glory worthiest;
If Christ were born in Burnley.

Christmas Day

EVELYN SHARP

'A Merry Christmas, a merry Christmas, a merry Christmas!' rang the Christmas bells across the snow.

Elfie kept her eyes shut tight, because she thought they were the fairy bells on the reindeer of Santa Claus; but Nancy sat up in bed and rubbed the sleep out of her eyes, and Pat suddenly gave a great shout. 'It's Christmas Day!' he cried; and, just as he said this, Baby marched in at the door of the night nursery, beating his new drum, and after that there was no more sleep for anybody.

'Merry Christmasses, merry Christmasses!' shouted Baby, and he hammered mightily on his drum till Nurse came and took it away from him.

'Come and play with your baker's cart instead,' she said coaxingly. 'That's a nice quiet toy.'

'I like loud toys best,' said Baby, and, finding that his drum was gone, he thumped the floor with his drum-stick instead. Fortunately, he was just of the height at which it did not make much difference to him whether he hit the floor or his new drum.

Christmas Day is the most beautiful day in the whole year on which to awake. It is ever so much better than a birthday, because only one person has presents on a birthday. It is like a birthday for the whole world, and that is why it makes everybody feel good and happy and jolly. It would be very difficult to feel cross on Christmas Day; and I never heard of anybody who quarrelled on it.

'Why are the bells ringing like that?' said Elfie.

'Like what?' asked Nancy, who was still rubbing her eyes.

'As if they were laughing,' said Elfie.

'I suppose they know it is Christmas Day,' said Nancy.

'Bells do not laugh,' said Nurse. 'Bells ring.'

'I think they laugh when they are Christmas bells,' said Elfie.

Christmas Day

NORA PERRY

What's this hurry, what's this flurry,
　All throughout the house today?
Everywhere a merry scurry.
　Everywhere a sound of play.
Something, too,'s the matter, matter,
　Out-of-doors as well as in,
For the bell goes clatter, clatter,
　Every minute – such a din!

Go and ask *them* what's the matter,
　What the fun outside and in –
What the meaning of the clatter,
　What the bustle and the din.
Hear them, hear them laugh and shout then,
　All together hear them say,
'Why, what have you been about, then,
　Not to know it's Christmas day?'

Father Christmas!
can you hear us,
calling up the
chimney wide?

Please take our wishes -
with your presents
to our friends this Christmas tide!

N H

'*Christmas Day is like a birthday for the whole world.*'

EVELYN SHARP

SING FOR XMAS

RING FOR XMAS

'I heard the bells on Christmas Day
Their old familiar carols play
And wild and sweet
The words repeat
Of Peace on earth, goodwill to men.'

H. W. LONGFELLOW

Now Thrice Welcome Christmas

ANON

Now thrice welcome, Christmas,
  Which brings us good cheer,
Minc'd pies and plum porridge,
  Good ale and strong beer;
With pig, goose, and capon,
  The best that can be,
So well doth the weather
  And our stomachs agree.

Observe how the chimneys
  Do smoke all about,
The cooks are providing
  For dinner no doubt;
For those on whose table
  No victuals appear,
O may they keep Lent
  All the rest of the year!

With holly and ivy
  So green and so gay,
We deck up our houses
  As fresh as the day,
With bays and rosemary,
  And laurel complete;
And every one now
  Is a king in conceit.

Wake Up!

(FREELY ADAPTED FROM THE OLD FRENCH BY
ELEANOR FARJEON)

Neighbour, what was the sound, I pray,
That did awake me as I lay
And to their doorways brought the people?
Every one heard it like a chime
Peeling for joy within a steeple:
    'Get up, good folk!
Get up, good folk, 'tis waking-time!'

Nay then, young Martin, know you not
That it is this our native spot
Sweet Love has chosen for his dwelling?
In every quarter rumours hum,
Rumours of news beyond all telling:
    'Wake up, good folk!
Wake up, good folk, for Christ is come.'

Neighbour, and is it really true,
True that the babe so small and new
Is lying even now among us?
What can we lay upon his knees
Of whose arrival angels sung us,
    What can we give,
What can we give the child to please?

Dickon shall bring a ball of silk,
Peter his son a pot of milk,
Colin a sparrow and a linnet,
Robin a cheese, and Ralph the half
Of a big cake with cherries in it,
    And jolly Jack
And jolly Jack a little calf.

I think this child will come to be
Some sort of workman such as we,
So he shall have my tools and chattels,
My well-set saw, my plane, my drill,
My hammer that so merry rattles,
    And planks of wood
And planks of wood to work at will.

When we have made our offerings.
Saying to him the little things
Whereof all babies born are witting,
Then we will take our leave and go,
Bidding good-night in manner fitting –
    So, so, wee lamb,
So, so, wee lamb, dream sweetly so.

And in a stable though he lies,
We in our hearts will soon devise
Such mansions as can never shame him.
There we will house and hold him dear,
And through the world to all proclaim him:
    'Wake up, good folk!
Wake up, good folk, for Christ is here.'

Christmas Mornings

Leonard Clark

Up in the morning early
sunlight on the cold floor,
nobody singing on far hills,
animals quiet, something in the air,
a touch of frost on the window sills.
a father standing by the door,
a mother smiling there,
a baby sleeping in the morning early.

Up in the morning, early
firelight on the warm floor,
everybody singing on the near hills,
whole house alive, something in the air,
a lick of rain on the window sills,
father standing by the door,
mother laughing there,
me waking in the morning early.

Carol of the Field Mice

KENNETH GRAHAME

Villagers all, this frosty tide,
Let your doors swing open wide,
Though wind may follow, and snow beside.
Yet draw us in by your fire to bide,
    Joy shall be yours in the morning!

Here we stand in the cold and the sleet.
Blowing fingers and stamping feet,
Come from far away you to greet –
You by the fire and we in the street –
    Bidding you joy in the morning!

For ere one half of the night was gone,
Sudden a star has led us on,
Raining bliss and benison –
Bliss tomorrow and more anon,
    Joy for every morning!

Goodman Joseph toiled through the snow –
Saw the star o'er a stable low;
Mary she might not further go –
Welcome thatch, and litter below!
    Joy was hers in the morning!

And then they heard the angels tell
'Who were the first to cry Nowell?
Animals all, as it befell,
In the stable where they did dwell!
    Joy shall be theirs in the morning!'

A Carol From the North of Spain

TRADITIONAL

Sing,
dance,
whisper along the way,
what shall we whisper?
It is Christmas day.

Sing,
dance,
what shall we bring?
Let no hand go empty
of gifts for the king

Sing,
dance,
a cake baked brown and sweet
Rosita brings
for Him to eat.

Sing,
dance,
Miguel brings a mouse
grey and small
for Christ's house.

Sing,
dance,
whisper along the way
What shall we whisper?
It is Christ's day.

Farmer Boy

LAURA INGALLS WILDER

Almanzo ducked and dodged and yelled, and threw snowballs as fast as he could, till they were all gone. Royal came charging over the wall with all the enemy after him, and Almanzo rose up and grabbed Frank. Headlong they went into the deep snow, outside the wall, and they rolled over and over, hitting each other as hard as they could.

Almanzo's face was covered with snow and his mouth was full of it, but he hung on to Frank and kept hitting at him. Frank's head hit his nose, and it began to bleed. Almanzo didn't care. He was on top of Frank, hitting him as hard as he could in the deep snow. He kept saying, 'Holler 'nuff! holler 'nuff!'

Frank grunted and squirmed. He rolled half over, and Almanzo got on top of him, He couldn't stay on top of Frank and hit him, so he bore down with all his weight, and he pushed Frank's face deeper and deeper into the snow.

And Frank gasped: ''Nuff!'

The Man They Made

HAMISH HENDRY

We made a Man all by ourselves;
  We made him jolly fat;
We stuck a Pipe into his face,
  And on his head a Hat.

We made him stand upon one Leg,
  That so he might not walk,
We made his Mouth without a Tongue,
  That so he might not talk.

We left him grinning on the Lawn
  That we to Bed might go;
But in the night he ran away –
  Leaving a heap of snow!

'Almanzo ducked and dodged and yelled and threw
snowballs as fast as he could . . .'

LAURA INGALLS WILDER

'Now ev'ry child that dwells on earth,
Stand up, stand up and sing.'

ELEANOR FARJEON

The Christmas Dinner

Evelyn Sharp

The Christmas dinner lasted a long while. This was not because people ate so much, but because it took the Squire so long to carve the turkey for everyone. But there was so much conversation going on, that no one noticed how long it took.

The great event of the dinner was the Christmas pudding. All the blinds were pulled down before it came in, which Baby did not like. 'Pull them up again,' he said. 'Don't want to go to bed.'

Then the pudding was brought in, all blazing with blue flames; and it was easy to see why the blinds had been pulled down. But Baby did not see why, and he was not happy till they were pulled up again. 'It isn't bed-time any more,' he said, beaming with smiles.

The best fun of all was trying to eat the blue flames as well as the pudding. It is not easy to eat blue flames in a spoon. But it is quite easy to think that one can; and that is much more important.

'I like eating flames,' said Pat. 'Flames taste of plums and currants and peel.'

'My flames taste of that, too,' said Cousin Bob; which made Pat feel very proud.

'You are not eating flames; you are just eating plum-pudding,' said Sylvia.

Nobody seemed to hear this remark of Cousin Sylvia's.

Under the Mistletoe

EVELYN SHARP

I've been standing here such a long time,' said Baby.

Nobody heard this remark at first, but when Baby repeated it at the top of his voice, everybody turned round. It is not usual, of course, to ask to be kissed under the mistletoe; but when the person who asks is very small, and has two big tears in his eyes, one forgets what is usual. So everybody in the room kissed Baby under the mistletoe, and the two big tears dried up and disappeared.

'I'm still standing under the mistletoe,' said Baby, when he had been kissed by everybody.

'A polite little boy does not stand too long under the mistletoe,' said Mother.

'I'm not a polite little boy,' said Baby; 'I like standing under mistletoes.'

For Them

Eleanor Farjeon

Before you bid, for Christmas' sake,
   Your guests to sit at meat.
Oh please to save a little cake
   For them that have no treat.

Before you go down party-dressed
   In silver gown or gold,
Oh please to send a little vest
   To them that still go cold.

Before you give your girl and boy
   Gay gifts to be undone,
Oh please to spare a little toy
   To them that will have none.

Before you gather round the tree
   To dance the day about,
Oh please to give a little glee
   To them that go without.

The Christmas Wish

Rose Fyleman

I went to the kitchen to stir the pudding –
   The Christmas pudding, the Christmas mince;
You never could guess what I saw on the table,
You never could guess . . . I haven't been able
   To settle to anything since.

She tasted a raisin, she tasted a currant,
   She flew to the basin's edge
And round and round she went merrily riding
And down the slippery sides a-gliding,
   Taking a fork for a sledge.

She stirred the pudding, I saw her do it,
   Using her silver shoe,
Then off she went by way of the dairy . . .
But think of our pudding *stirred by a fairy!*
   Can it, oh, can it be true?

Pudding Charms

Charlotte Druitt Cole

Our Christmas pudding was made in November,
All they put in it, I quite well remember:
Currants and raisins, and sugar and spice,
Orange peel, lemon peel – everything nice
Mixed up together, and put in a pan.
'When you've stirred it,' said Mother, 'as much as you can.
We'll cover it over, that nothing may spoil it,
And then, in the copper, tomorrow we'll boil it.'
That night, when we children were all fast asleep,
A real fairy godmother came crip-a-creep!

She wore a red cloak, and a tall steeple hat
(Though nobody saw her but Tinker, the cat!)
And out of her pocket a thimble she drew,
A button of silver, a silver horse-shoe,
And, whisp'ring a charm, in the pudding pan popped them,
Then flew up the chimney directly she dropped them;
And even old Tinker pretended he slept
(With Tinker a secret is sure to be kept!)
So nobody knew, until Christmas came round,
And there, in the pudding, these treasures we found.

Christmas Plum Pudding

CLIFTON BINGHAM

When they sat down that day to dine
The beef was good, the turkey fine
But oh, the pudding!

The goose was tender and so nice,
That everybody had some twice –
But oh, that pudding!

It's coming, that they knew quite well,
They didn't see, they couldn't smell,
That fine plum pudding!

It came, an object of delight!
Their mouths watered at the sight
Of that plum pudding!

When they had finished, it was true,
They'd also put a finish to
That poor plum pudding!

CHARLESROBINSON

The Pantomime

Evelyn Sharp

'Tomorrow,' said Mother, looking mysterious, 'something is going to happen.'

'Something nice or something nasty?' asked several voices.

'I wonder which you would call it,' said Mother, thoughtfully.

But anybody could see from the look in the corner of her eye that she knew it was something people would wish to happen.

'Oh, Mother!' gasped Elfie. 'Is it – is it the pantomime?'

Mother nodded. 'Cinderella,' she said.

All the children screamed and danced for joy when they heard this, from superior Cousin Bob down to Baby.

'I've seen four pantomimes,' said superior Cousin Bob. 'I hope this one will be good.'

'Hooray!' shouted Baby. 'We're going to have a pantymime!'

Then he whispered to Nancy, who always knew everything and never laughed at him, 'Please, is it something to eat or to drink?'

The Demons

EVELYN SHARP

The pantomime began with the demons. 'Pantomimes always begin with demons,' said superior Cousin Bob.

'Why?' asked Baby.

Cousin Bob did not know. 'Listen to the pantomime,' he said.

'I wish they didn't begin with demons,' said Baby.

The pantomime people must have heard this, for the demons suddenly went down a hole, and the lights went up.

Between the Acts

Evelyn Sharp

Why have they pulled down the blind?' asked Baby, when the curtain fell at the end of the Prince's ball.

'It will begin again soon,' said Father.

'Will it begin all over again from the beginning?' asked Elfie, who thought that anything could happen in Fairyland.

'It is easy to see that you have never been to a pantomime before,' chuckled Cousin Bob.

Elfie wondered why this was so easy to see, and she tried to return the compliment.

'It is easy to see that you have been to four pantomimes, Cousin Bob,' she said politely.

Father laughed very much at this; but Cousin Bob did not seem so much amused.

'Have they gone to bed behind the blind? I wish they'd wake up. I want some more!' shouted Baby, impatiently.

Immediately, the curtain went up again. Baby was very pleased with himself.

'I have woke the pantomime up,' he said.

The Harlequin

EVELYN SHARP

'Who is that man dressed like a cracker?' asked Nancy.

'That is the harlequin,' explained Mother.

'Why doesn't the clown catch him when he hits him with that funny strap?' asked Pat, knowing from experience what would happen to him if he came up behind anybody with a strap.

'The clown cannot see him,' said Mother. 'Nobody can see him. He is invisible.'

'Somebody can see him,' mentioned Baby. 'I can see him.'

'They cannot see him on the stage,' explained Mother.

'Shall we tell them when we see him coming?' asked Baby, eagerly.

'Certainly not,' said Father, in a great hurry. 'It would spoil the fun.'

'I don't think it would spoil the fun,' said Baby. 'I think, perhaps, they would like to know.'

Father was quite sure they would not like to know, and Cousin Bob declared that people never did these things at pantomimes; so Baby contented himself with giving Father a big dig in the back with Grandmamma's umbrella, which was about the size of a small tent.

'I'm invisible,' said Baby with a smile, when Father turned round.

'That's lucky for you,' said Father. And he kept hold of Grandmamma's umbrella for the rest of the afternoon.

Boxing Day

Evelyn Sharp

'Why is it called Boxing Day?' asked Baby.

'Because it is the day we give people their Christmas boxes,' said father. 'Look! There is the postman; run and give him his Christmas box.'

All this was very puzzling to Baby; but he did what he was told, and stood on tiptoe and gave the postman his Christmas box. 'Though it isn't a box really,' he added apologetically; 'it's just pennies.' The postman did not mind this; he liked pennies best.

'The poor postman deserves his Christmas box,' said Mother. 'He has to go out in all weathers to take people their letters.'

'I should like to be the poor postman,' said Baby, 'The poor postman can stamp in the puddles all day long.'

'I expect the postman is tired of stamping in puddles,' said Mother. Baby thought this highly improbable.

A MERRY CHRISTMAS,
& A HAPPY NEW YEAR.

'*Villagers all, this frosty tide,*
Let your doors swing open wide.'

KENNETH GRAHAME

'Greetings, good master, mistress, children,
Greetings, good health, to one and all!'

RUTH HELLER

Boxing Day

Mary Clive

I have often noticed that one feels rather flat on Boxing Day. The weather is generally grey and dull, and children are apt to be tired and bored.

'I can't think why it is,' said Rosamund, 'I don't really like these sweets at all now, and yet I just can't stop eating them.'

'My mouth feels all sugary inside,' I said, 'I wonder if one of those lumps of nougat would take the taste away.'

I took one but it was horrid, and when I tried to throw it in the fire it hit the fender. It became very runny and stuck in the wire meshes, and the more we tried to poke it through with a pencil the more sticky everything became.

'You'd better not have any more sweets, Harry,' said Rosamund, 'not after what happened at dinner.'

Harry appeared to be pondering great thoughts. At last he spoke.

'Sick can be very surprising sometimes.'

'Well, we certainly were more surprised than pleased,' said Rosamund. 'Why did you say that you were too hungry to eat?'

'Because I thought I was,' said Harry humbly.

69

New Year's Morning

Evelyn Sharp

'I'm a year older than I was last night, I am!' shouted Baby, as he went into the breakfast-room with the others to kiss Mother.

'So is everybody,' said Father. 'I have two new grey hairs.'

Baby stood and looked at him carefully, when he said this. 'What have you done with the old ones, Daddy?' he asked. 'Did the Old Year take them away?'

'I hope so,' laughed Father.

'The Old Year has not taken away your grey hairs, Grandpapa,' said Baby. 'Except the ones on the top,' he added.

'Hush!' said Mother. 'You should not say anything about people's looks, Baby. It is rude to make personal remarks.'

'Come here, Baby, and let me put your hair tidy,' said Nancy, to change the conversation.

'Oh, Nancy!' said Baby, in a shocked tone. 'It is very rude to make personable remarks.'

Welcome to the New Year

ELEANOR FARJEON

Hey, my lad! ho, my lad!
 Here's a New Broom.
Heaven's your housetop
 And Earth is your room.

Tuck up your shirt-sleeves,
 There's plenty to do –
Look at the muddle
 That's waiting for you!

Dust in the corners
 And dirt on the floor,
Cobwebs still clinging
 To window and door.

Hey, my lad! ho, my lad!
 Nimble and keen –
Here's your New Broom, my lad!
 See you sweep clean.

Greetings, good master, mistress, children

RUTH HELLER

Greetings, good master, mistress, children,
    Greetings, good health to one and all!
Once more we come to you with singing,
    Open your door, we've come to call.
        Let us now to your hearth draw near,
        With warmth and with food let us be welcomed:
Greetings, good master, mistress, children,
    We hope our songs will bring good cheer.
We wish you all a merry Christmas
    And a most happy New Year.

Greeting, good master, mistress, children,
    If our singing does not please,
We shall not be the least offended,
    Though you now leave us here to freeze.
        Far we have travelled on this day
        To sing and to bring the season's greetings.
Therefore, good master, mistress, children,
    Will you now kindly lend an ear?
Let us wish you a merry Christmas
    And a most happy New Year.

The Little Match Girl

Hans Christian Andersen

It was dreadfully cold, the snow fell thick and fast and it was almost dark. The last evening of the old year was drawing in. But, cold and dark as it was, a poor little girl with bare head and feet was still wandering about the streets. When she left home she had slippers on but they were much too large for her, for they really belonged to her mother, and they had dropped off her feet when she was running very quickly across the road to get out of the way of two carriages. One of the slippers couldn't be found and the other had been snatched up by a little boy, who ran off with it.

So now the little girl walked on, her bare feet quite blue with cold. She carried a small bundle of matches in her hand and a good many more in her tattered apron. No one had bought any of them the whole day – no one had given her a single penny. Trembling with cold and hunger, she crept on, looking the picture of sorrow.

The snowflakes fell on her long, fair hair, which curled in pretty ringlets over her shoulders, but she wasn't thinking about her own beauty or of the cold. Lights were glimmering through every window, and the smell of roast goose reached her from several houses; it was New Year's eve, and it was this that she was thinking about.

She sat down in the corner of two houses, drawing her little feet close under her, but in vain, for she couldn't warm them up. She dared not go home as she hadn't sold any matches and perhaps her father would beat her. Besides, her home was almost as cold as the street: it was an attic, and although the largest of many chinks in the roof were stopped up with straw and rags, the wind and snow often came through. Her hands were nearly dead with cold; perhaps one little match from her bundle would warm them, if she dared light it. She drew one out, and struck it against the wall. It was a bright, warm flame, and she held her hands over it. For a moment there was something magic about it and it seemed to her as though she were sitting before a large iron stove with brass ornaments. The fire burnt so brightly that the child stretched out her feet to warm them too. Alas! in a moment the flame had died away, the stove vanished and the little girl sat cold and comfortless again with the burnt match in her hand.

She struck a second match against the wall; it kindled and blazed, and wherever its light fell the wall became transparent like glass. The little girl could see into the room within. She saw a table spread with a snow-like damask cloth and covered with shining china dishes. The roast goose stuffed with apples and dried plums stood at one end, smoking hot, and – which was best of all to see – the goose, jumped down from the dish, and waddled along the floor as though he were coming right up to the poor child. The match was burnt out, and only the thick hard wall was beside her.

She kindled a third match. Again the flame shot up – and now she was sitting under a most beautiful Christmas-tree, far larger and far more prettily decked out than the one she had seen last Christmas Eve through the door of a rich merchant's house. Hundreds of wax tapers lit up the green branches and tiny painted figures, such as she had seen in the shop windows, looked down from the tree. The child stretched out her hands in delight, and in that moment the light of the match was quenched. Still, however, the Christmas candles burned higher and higher – she saw them shining like stars in heaven. One of them fell, the light streaming behind it like a long, fiery tail.

'Some one is dying,' said the little girl softly, for her old grandmother – the only person who had ever been kind to her and who had died long ago – had told her that whenever a star falls, an immortal spirit returns to the God who gave it.

She struck yet another match against the wall; it flamed up and there appeared before her that same dear grandmother, surrounded by its light.

Happy Christmas to you.

'The snow fell on her long hair which curled in pretty ringlets over her shoulders but she wasn't thinking about her own beauty or of the cold.'

H. C. ANDERSEN

'We'll take a cup of kindness yet
For the sake of Auld Lang Syne.'

ROBERT BURNS

She looked gentle and loving as she always had done, but now she was bright and happy too.

'Grandmother!' cried the child, 'oh, take me with you! I know you will leave me as soon as the match goes out – you will vanish like the warm fire in the stove, like the splendid New Year's feast, like the beautiful large Christmas-tree,' and she hastily lit all the remaining matches in the bundle, lest her grandmother should disappear. They burned with such a blaze of splendour that noon-day could scarcely have been brighter. Never had the good old grandmother looked so tall and stately, so beautiful and kind. She took the little girl in her arms, and they flew together – joyfully and gloriously they flew – higher and higher, till they were at last in Paradise, where neither cold, nor hunger, nor pain, is ever known.

But in the cold morning hour, crouching in the corner of the wall, the poor little girl was found – her cheeks glowing, her lips smiling – frozen to death on the last night of the Old Year. The New Year's sun shone on the lifeless child; motionless she sat there with the matches in her lap, one bundle of which was quite burnt out.

'She has been trying to warm herself, poor thing!' the people said; but no one knew the sweet visions she had seen, or how gloriously she and her grandmother were celebrating their New Year's festival.

Up the Hill
Down the Hill

Eleanor Farjeon

Old One, lie down
Your journey is done
Little New Year
Will rise with the sun
Now you have come to
The foot of the hill
Lay down your bones
Old year and lie still.

Young one step out
Your journey's begun
Weary old year
Makes way for his son
Now you have started
I climb up the hill
Put best foot forward
New year, with a will.

Father Time